MARK WELL MY WORDS

Liston Monsanto, Sr.

authorHOUSE®

AuthorHouse™
1663 Liberty Drive
Bloomington, IN 47403
www.authorhouse.com
Phone: 1-800-839-8640

First published by AuthorHouse 5/24/2010

ISBN: 978-1-4490-8971-9 (e)
ISBN: 978-1-4490-8975-7 (sc)

Printed in the United States of America
Bloomington, Indiana

This book is printed on acid-free paper.

Beloved: "Where jealousy and selfish ambitions exist, there is disorder and every foul practice. But the wisdom from above is first of all pure, then peaceable, gentle, compliant, full of mercy and good fruits without inconstancy or insincerity."

James 3:16

DEDICATION

Under most circumstances I would dedicate this book to a person or persons living dignified lives, but since we have continued on the course chartered by Governor Melvin H. Evans in 1970, I feel duty bound to say: For their success in shifting our attention from failure to lead by example to crimes of violence and for their success in placing a mark of disgrace on the young miscreants in the United States Virgin Islands who are now attempting to become genocidal, I dedicate this book to all corrupted wrongdoers in the United States Virgin Islands, whose corruptness continues to be celebrated by disadvantaged people.

PREFACE

Inasmuch as over the past fifty years (although displaying the note of scholarship), many of the books written by Virgin Islanders have had embodied within them much information relating cautiously to the unusual events that have formed our lifestyle, as a straitlaced nationalist, a prude and an erudite person whose authority to write this book has been derived from those meritorious attributes and inasmuch as it matters not to the aristocrats and business people (as they continue to finance the political campaigns of local politicians hoping for a quid pro quo) who our elected leaders are, nor does it worry the many degenerates and hirelings who continue to suffer from the virus of fear while simultaneously being fed crumbs from the political table in our corrupted and less-than-professional governmental system, as explicit as I am and as a person devoted to the welfare of all human beings I find myself in a very good position to write a book that deviates from the norm while at the same time serving as a counterbalance.

And so today, writing as a man of principle with an enviable record, I begin the preface of this book entitled *"Mark Well My Words"* by saying that some people have college degrees (résumés) which are extinguished simultaneously with their deaths. Others have records which outlive them so that the living may be afforded the opportunity of using those same records as case law.

I -- Liston B. Monsanto, Sr., having defeated the United States Virgin Islands Governmental System through Opinion Number 81-1434 of the Third Circuit Court of Appeals in Philadelphia, Pennsylvania, and thereafter having the courage of my convictions to live in the selfsame U.S. Virgin Islands' undisciplined society where just about everyone (from the top down) operates in violation of law -- am compelled to use my instructive experience to encourage and/or warn my compatriots that it is high time for everybody in the U.S. Virgin Islands to be altruistic enough in working for the welfare of his fellow man. And so it is for this and other reasons that I'm supremely happy to say that when it comes to sharing the contents of this book with my inquiring readers, I need very little persuasion.

The existing lifestyle in the United States Virgin Islands has influenced the people's present behavior to an abnormal degree. Through political patronage and cronyism they have become indentured to an archaic system which has within it much fondness for ease, thereby transforming them from industrious people to first-class hirelings, social climbers, and kleptomaniacs. Sadly to say, they are without knowledge of when loyalty ends and when slavery begins.

In my time on the job (40 years as a civil servant) I made enemies with members of the power-elite due largely to my respect for law and authority. Unlike a whole lot of our college graduates who look at professionalism with disapproval, I (after being exposed to a high degree of professionalism as a member of the United States Air Force and later after being trained by the United States Internal Revenue Service) immediately lost my taste for ignorance.

This I say, cognizant of the fact that due to education and hypocrisy, many of our college graduates are living a treacherous academic life. Because most of our denizens (in our small U.S. Virgin Islands communities) are related either by blood or through marriage, the college graduates find it too big a proposition to visibly separate themselves from unlettered people and underachievers who are of the belief that a college degree automatically makes a person intelligent. With treachery hidden under a veneer of friendship and unknown to many of the underachievers and unlettered people, the college graduates try hard not to give an appearance of superior quality in spuriously associating with people not on their educational level. As members of the world of scholars covertly showing off an exaggerated feeling of superiority, they have within their ranks a high degree of jealousy. On the highest rung of the academic ladder sits the PhD looking down on everybody while the holder of the MA makes subordinate the holder of the BA who in turn looks down on the remainder men. Put simply, in the United Sates Virgin Islands where we live, academic life is displayed somewhat ostentatiously and permeates down through the ranks.

Without a centralized educational complex and without an institution of higher learning during the roaring twenties leading up to the thirties when the Charlotte Amalie High School graduated its first class, were I called upon to write this book and all the others that I've written, I would have had to communicate with most of my uneducated and unlettered readers (who were without systematic training and learning) through a literal account written in its simplest form. Today, however, with elementary and secondary schools plus the University of the Virgin Islands, I find it a most facile task to stray from yesterday's standards and principles in exposing the many hustlers, con men, and oppressors in language that most modern day people understand.

This book, like a buffet, offers a smorgasbord of digestive material designed to shed light on a U.S. Virgin Islands unorthodox lifestyle with the spotlight on many of the people for whom monuments have been named and many others for whom testimonials were extended as a token of esteem, admiration, and gratitude. As a reader eager to know what's taking place in our repressive U.S. Virgin Islands Government, surely you must know that reading can extend one's knowledge. What you might not know, however, is that you can improve your reading still more if you try reading *"Mark Well My Words."*

CHAPTER I

Truth And Occurences

I write fully cognizant of the fact that my imagination is so limited that it makes it a most difficult task for me to know how to lie. That is not to say that I've got a monopoly on the truth, but when it comes to taking on the politicians together with their spin doctors and the many political pundits who are always politically correct in the United States Virgin Islands, non-partisan as I am, I'm free to use my First Amendment right to rake over the coals many of the people responsible for where the U.S. Virgin Islands are today.

There is a great worry over what's happening in the U.S. Virgin Islands. Our political leaders and many of the people in positions of authority are not adept at living by the rule of law -- a fact corroborated by former Governor Alexander A. Farrelly in his State of the Territory Address on Friday, January 16, 1987. Farrelly said: "The state of the territorial government is deplorable. I believe it is charitable to describe the government that I now head as being in a shambles: bankrupt in its legal meaning, dispirited, often in violation of law, and operating often without rhyme or reason, benefiting neither the persons for whom services are to be provided nor fairly and fully compensating those who are to provide the services."

In point of fact, it must be noted that the U.S. Virgin Islands were acquired from Denmark on March 31, 1917. And by virtue of that acquisition, the United States was given a legal right to the Islands which upon consummation of the sale immediately fell under the kindly guidance of the United States Constitution. In the United States and locally within the naval administration which governed the Islands for fourteen years from the date of the acquisition, white supremacy and segregation were the order of the day. Contrary to the many anti-American sentiments being spread by way of innuendo, the truth is the United States did not buy the inhabitants and no attempt was made to chase them away from the Islands. As a matter of fact, the inhabitants were given a ten-year period (1917-1927) in which to make a decision with respect to residency and citizenship. The men were even permitted to join the United States Navy.

After carefully weighing the advantages against the disadvantages of U.S. ownership, on page 16 of my book *"Perpetuating the Memory of a Sportscaster,"* briefly I wrote: "As far as I'm concerned, the best thing to have ever taken place in the United States Virgin Islands was that day in 1917 when the purchase of the U.S. Virgin Islands was consummated. Had the United States bought at random Antigua, Nevis, or St. Kitts, many of us who call ourselves native Virgin Islanders today may have been born on one of those islands. Our parents may have migrated there for reasons of economics in much the same way as people from those islands are coming to the United States Virgin Islands today. We should consider ourselves fortunate, especially the passive St. Thomians, who, because of a fine harbor, were born on third base ninety feet from home plate."

The acquisition brought with it a call for much allegiance to the United States on the part of the Islands' inhabitants. Beginning in 1931 until 1970, civilian governors were appointed by the various presidents of the United States. And what's more, included in the school's curriculum was the Pledge of Allegiance to the Flag of the United States and the singing of patriotic songs. Outside the regular course of study, the children of school age were given largess in the form of gift boxes from the American Red Cross. And as if that was not enough, large-sized pianos were distributed to many of the local people and as destitute as we were during the period, we were supremely happy to share in the New Deal program, which had within it the Civilian Conservation Corp, or C/C Camp as it was called locally.

On federal holidays such as Memorial Day and Independence Day, the inhabitants were treated to military parades – all designed to win their love and loyal support for the United States of America.

As an overseas territorial possession, Virgin Islanders were granted immunity from the many hardships and handicaps endured by African Americans on the mainland. Living on our tiny Islands with a paucity of white people, freedom of movement was very much in vogue. Furthermore, it is a matter of record and not an exaggerated statement that Virgin Islanders were never enslaved by the United States. The country from which the United States acquired the Islands (Denmark) abolished slavery in the Islands on July 3, 1848. It was sixty-nine years later when the United States took possession of the Islands. During that interim period, except for the freedom gained in 1848, everything remained status quo. What's strange is that under Denmark, Danish was not taught in the school system. English was then and continues to be our primary language, making it easy to communicate with the Americans. Today by way of being magnanimous and through reconciliation, many locals have seen it fit to form an organization they fondly refer to as the "Friends of Denmark." Many former British colonies in the Caribbean who are now independent and whose land area in square miles is much larger than the U.S. Virgin Islands continue to see an exodus of their citizens leaving their respective island and establishing residency in the U.S. Virgin Islands. Why? Because of the United States flag that flies over the Islands, thereby giving them the opportunity to make the Protestant ethic pay dividends. Unlike countries independent of the control of other governments, the U.S. Virgin Islands under existing conditions must rely on the United States for its survival. Put simply, the U.S. Virgin Islands are an unincorporated territorial possession of the United States.

Presently the U.S. Virgin Islands are the only place under the American flag with a government that's filled to the brim with totalitarian principles. Through political patronage, cronyism, and political ineptitude, the citizens find themselves under the leadership of a number of repressors, who for the most part were elected by them, to lead the Islands.

At this juncture I'm going to bring your attention back to the many people making up our citizenry. When the many naturalized citizens made their exodus from the former British colonies in the eastern Caribbean, they were relegated to menial work and berated through words of contempt by hostile citizens whose claim to fame was the fact that they were born in the Virgin Islands. Because of a high degree of ethnocentrism and egocentrism (their common responsibilities and interest notwithstanding) they were splintered into dissenting groups, finding it a most difficult task to vote for a candidate not belonging to the island whence they came. As fellowmen they would socialize with each other. But with the passage of time, due largely to hard work and an operational doctrine which had within it information on solidarity and the advantages of unity over division, they would become a friendly Trojan horse in our midst by unifying themselves into a solid voting bloc, thereby becoming associate members of every elected governor's administration. Suffering from political ineptitude, false pride, xenophobia, lack of leadership, and lack of foresight while at the same time being exploited by a multitude of shysters locally, the ancestral natives and native Virgin Islanders -- who themselves were splintered into dissenting groups in a Virgin Islands repressive governmental system --unknowingly surrendered the Islands to the naturalized citizens.

It is for the foregoing reasons that I'm of the belief that until and unless we become politically mature (a prima facie fact known to the powers that be in the United States) we'll never get the chance to vote in the United States presidential elections. I furthermore believe that Virgin Islanders are standing in the path of progress via their attitudes. Finally, let me end by saying that inasmuch as all U.S. territorial possessions operate on a silent motto of "All for one and one for all," everybody in the various territories is affected and therefore denied the opportunity to vote for president. In short, if one gets it, all get it. A word to the wise is therefore sufficient: In order to avoid being charged with open intervention into the affairs of the Virgin Islands and, furthermore, getting mixed up in local politics, the United States will never tell us how abrasive our attitudes are. Consequently, I reiterate my contention thusly: we cannot have growth in the U.S. Virgin Islands without changed attitudes.

And since I'm offering my take on voting for President of the United States, not to be remiss, I'm now forced to say, somewhat succinctly, that following the acquisition of the Islands from Denmark and the establishment of a military government under the control of the United States Navy, many of our men (out of work and desirous of seeing the world) joined the United States Navy of their own volition – most prominent among them was bandmaster Alton A. Adams the first (writer and arranger of the Virgin Islands March – a march currently serving as our National Anthem). The point that I'm making here especially for those people critical of the United States for having us defend the nation and its territories as members of the military while denying us the right to vote for President is that the United States did not force the men of the Virgin Islands into becoming conscripted soldiers or sailors. It was people of prominence in the Territory who made the impassioned speech asking that the Virgin Islands be included in the selective service system.

Because the American flag flies over the U.S. Virgin Islands and because mercantile St. Thomas (the Hub) and industrial St. Croix have become the playground for the

Caribbean, people are leaving the various islands (large and small) in droves where they already have complete control over their own affairs and taking up residency in the United States Virgin Islands. They are not coming to the U.S. Virgin Islands to vote for a status of independence. If they wanted independence they would have stayed in their native lands. Put simply, they are coming to the Virgin Islands for reasons of economics, while at the same time filling the void created by U.S. Virgin Islanders, many of whom preferred to run away rather than introduce innovations into a U.S. Virgin Islands totalitarian government. Having sold out the Virgin Islands through condescension and a thirst for politics, grief stricken as we have become, our only comfort in grief lies in the fact that the offspring of the many immigrants and naturalized citizens who were born and raised in the United Sates Virgin Islands will one day, through bequeathal, own a large part of the Caribbean as citizens of the United States.

While the Earth continues to rotate on its axis and while (for the purpose of making this point) many of the inhabitants of the former British colonies in the eastern Caribbean are displaying changed attitudes through education, here in the U.S. Virgin Islands through the usage of a modus operandi, many people (from the highest levels of government downward) continue to be at variance with the facts while employing isolationist policies through a strategy of divide and conquer. Before we can move forward together as a people, we must accept the fact that the U.S. Virgin Islands are a territorial possession of the United States. They are not ours. Look at the deed. Under present conditions, in order to move forward we must have the blessings of the United States. And this, folks, brings me to the issue of culture.

At the outset let me say that ours is a cosmopolitan society wherein there are many people of diverse interest paying taxes, voting, and making positive contributions to our economic growth. No ethnic group has the legal right to force its cultural traits on another. As concerns African descendants, let me say that through education our schools are designed to change a major part of our culture, especially when it comes to reading, writing, and doing sums. Reciting through recitations is designed to test our memories while at the same time prepare us for public speaking. In school, for example, we are taught that the word "pot" is not pronounced "pat" and that the word "what" is not pronounced "wah."

We speak in the vernacular to each other at any time, and, limited as my education is, when called upon to write for the record, or furthermore to the same people with whom I have established rapport, I immediately apply the lessons learned in school.

This I can do owing to the fact that I'm not canvassing for votes. Many people, most of whom are engaged in politics locally, refuse to make allowances for the wishes of others that they use the vernacular when appropriate.

One day while operating as a taxicab driver, I became fortunate enough to pick up three newsmen from NBC in the vicinity of the Emancipation Garden in downtown Charlotte Amalie. They instructed me to drive them to Havensight where their cruise ship was at anchor. En route to the ship they asked me to pick up one of their supposedly wayward colleagues who had left them and begun walking to the ship. About fifty yards away from the Emancipation Garden I spotted the errant newsman carrying a tripod. I pulled up beside him and beckoned him to climb into the car, whereupon I learned in the conversation that followed that he was born and raised in the state of Louisiana where a southern drawl was part of his vernacular. He went on to say, however, that because of the nature of his work he was told by the powers that be at NBC to drop the Louisiana drawl while broadcasting. At first he said it was a most difficult task making the conversion from his vernacular to the preferred language of NBC, but with the flight of time he overcame the challenge and became bilingual. The moral of the story is, there is a time and place for everything.

There was a time in the U.S. Virgin Islands when the only musical instrument in our elementary public school system was a piano. It was purposefully put in the schools as an accompaniment for the young pupils, thereby making it easy for them to learn the various songs that they would be required to sing. Favored by circumstances, the older students at the Charlotte Amalie High School were fortunate enough to have brasses, percussions, strings, and woodwinds -- all designed to aid them in uniting as a group to form a band. The foregoing said, I now make this point which I've considered most salient. In today's U.S. Virgin Islands society we have in our high schools all the musical instruments previously listed plus a number of steel bands that perform here, there, and everywhere. Incidentally, we also have the University of the V.I. band and the National Guard's band. So now what's missing? A community band! Folks, it is not that I'm being critical. I just wanted to leave the impress of my personality on what I'm writing especially as it relates to culture and the fact that culture is a changing thing. The lancers, the Virginia reel, and the minuet were all done during the month of May in St. Thomas with the community band providing the music. But that was yesterday. In today's U.S. Virgin Islands during our annual Carnival activities when we get our chance to put on display our culture, calypso leads the way. We promote calypso via competition in our calypso tents and in all the Carnival parades. Ninety-nine percent of the music being played by the participating bands is calypso. Quelbé lovers like myself have to be told that our changing times bring with it a change in culture. This, therefore, begs the question with respect to what is really the official music of the U.S. Virgin Islands. So taking into consideration what you have just read and knowing that the U.S. Virgin Islands are the only place under the American flag where people are afraid to speak out inasmuch as they dread losing jobs, the results of a secret survey show that naming quelbé the official music of the U.S.V.I. has disquieted a number of people. Here now for your enlightenment are some of the things having to do with our culture that have changed or otherwise become obsolete: (a) our traditional handshake has changed somewhat, (b) kalaloo prepared once a year (New Year's Eve called "Old Year's Night" locally) is now an everyday meal, (c) Night Soil program phased out, replaced by modern day toilets, (d) donkeys replaced by motor vehicles, (e) reservoirs condemned and replaced by desalination plants, (f) Mom & Pop stores (shops) replaced by supermarkets, (g) coal pots replaced by stoves, (h) blaming children today for parents' failure to provide guidance, and (i) replacing Mr., Mrs., and Miss with profanity in our mass culture. Everything with the exception of the people's attitude is changing for the better. The masses have refused to be a part of a modern world through blatant hypocrisy.

As an afterthought, I would like to say that when, in the United States or any other territorial possession, Virgin Islanders must speak standard English as a means of engaging in meaningful dialogue with people outside of their ethnic group. The ability to switch from our vernacular to what we call "yanking" is a talent that a lot of people do not possess. Yanking is nothing to be ashamed of. Ponder this: write an essay using standard English. Read it aloud. Pass it on to a Yankee and have him read it aloud. Sounds different doesn't it? In the U.S. Virgin Islands because of jealousy, envy, etc. it's always open season on each other when we try to do the right thing. U.S. Virgin Islanders Tim Duncan (professional basketball player and Wake Forest graduate) and professional singer John Lucien (now deceased) both profited from being able to "yank" while speaking standard English.

In the U.S. Virgin Islands it is with freedom of speech through tendentious statements that a person can assail the atrocities committed by Benito Mussolini (leader of the Italian fascists) and Adolph Hitler (dictator of Germany) two good for nothings who died in 1945, but when it comes to that same person seeking to express his concerns regarding the many evil taskmasters in the U.S. Virgin Islands government (living or dead) who take tremendous pride in showing a high degree of inconsideration for their subordinates, he's charged with going to extremes. In protecting the good for nothings, the spin doctors and political pundits are always quick to evade the point by twisting the meaning of bad towards good and the meaning of lie towards truth. They will say never mind, they (the evil taskmasters) are united in the same league with Hitler and Mussolini; these people although degenerates are to be revered as they are serving as role models for our children. Look at the many monuments bearing their names.

In the United States Virgin Islands there is a high degree of defalcation. Time after time, money entrusted to people has been misused. During my tenure as an employee of the Virgin Islands Bureau of Internal Revenue, anarchy became rampant. The Disclosure Law was enforced to the point where it became a hindrance to free speech inasmuch as it was not being used for its intended purpose. Tacitly incorporated in the Disclosure Law is the Bureau's guiding principle which says: "While in fools paradise, one must hear no evil, see no evil, or speak no evil. Cooperate with the assembled gentry in doing lots of evil herein." This principle is enforced to the hilt in order to protect those at the highest levels in the organizational structure who have become corrupted through deceitful desires.

And now that I have arrived at the final part of this chapter, I'd like to ask that the language used herein not be construed as a maneuver for some advantage over the Virgin Islands governmental system or a gambit that's designed to outwit or puzzle anyone.

On the Virgin Islands commemorative quarter recently minted and issued by the governmental authority of the United States, there is an inscription on the back of the coin that has been adopted by the people of the Virgin Islands and serves as our motto. The inscription reads: "United in Pride and Hope." This motto was presumably designed to mislead people not familiar with the lifestyle in the United States Virgin Islands, or better yet to inspire and ask Virgin Islanders to undergo a complete metamorphosis. Due largely to politics, it has become the habitual tendency of Virgin Islanders to reverse the standards of right and wrong. We are not a prideful people. Were we united in pride, we'd be voting for President of the United States.

At last check, our false pride was put on display when Edward E. Thomas (CEO at WICO) was honored in the wake of his wicked deeds, which are detailed in Chapter IV of "The Extreme Test."

Mr. Thomas, as director at the Virgin Islands Bureau of Internal Revenue, found himself at the highest level of the organizational structure. The record shows that he often operated in violation of the law. Mr. Thomas demonstrated to the readers of "The Extreme Test" that he has no pride. Given the choice of accepting or rejecting the offer, he accepted, knowing that the sponsoring organization would applaud wrong.

At this juncture, not wanting to dwell on the matter of pride as it relates to Mr. Edward E. Thomas, I ask that you consider carefully the following questions: Why don't we show respect for the National Anthem when it is being sung or played? Why is much emphasis placed on profanity throughout the island and within earshot of locals and visitors alike? Why do we have so many vagrants in our tourist-oriented society? There is no need to go any further with my questions.

In conclusion, I'd like to say however that when it comes to being prideful in the Virgin Islands, it's all false. And so you may ask with good reason: why the straightforwardness? The simple answer is, I have what many people in the Virgin Islands may consider weakness – I'm moralistic.

CHAPTER II

THE SCOFFLAWS

Surrealistic as it seems, in the United States Virgin Islands the unwritten policy of "Security and Safety in Numbers takes precedence over lawfulness" has been our vehicle of thought. Our laws have been relegated to a position of dormancy while unrestrained scofflaws are allowed to run wild and wooly.

Over the last thirty years the usage of arbitrary power and a penchant for breaking laws have triumphed over existing laws. Our elected officials at the highest levels are very much aware of the many infractions but, because they themselves are scofflaws who must rely on a law-breaking people for votes, there is no antipathy against it. That being the case, those in whom the authority is vested and therefore charged with the responsibility of providing security and safety for the masses as permitted by law have thrown a wet blanket over existing laws, and in keeping with what they have secretly labeled a most prudent policy are privately saying: "To hell with the law; everybody's doing it wrong and that means that it's right."

What the common people, the working classes, and the lower classes of society do not understand is that when they become aggrieved finding themselves in an awkward position they must resort to the courts for help, where inevitably they'll find themselves going up against the same guidelines (which include the V.I. Code) that they were allowed to violate from the inception of their employment. All of a sudden they'll see and hear lawyers from the Attorney General's office showing off before the court, putting sophistry on display to the detriment of the aggrieved. They will make a great show citing their authority under the V.I. Code in a glaring attempt to rid the government of an uninformed grievant. This is what goes on in the Virgin Islands where you have a number of government employees (some labeled functional illiterates) who cannot think for themselves. Lest you forget, the mantra among the scofflaws in positions of authority is: Keep the people in ignorance while perpetuating yourself in office.

That they are breaking the laws of the Virgin Islands with impunity is evidenced by Opinion Number 81-1434 (United States Court of Appeals for the Third Circuit), the details of which appear in a book authored by me entitled "The Extreme Test." This book exposes to the reader exactly what law-breaking activities took place at the Virgin Islands Bureau of Internal Revenue (the income-producing arm of the government wherein the sword of Damocles hangs threateningly over the heads of the employees though a disclosure law) during my forty-year tenure as an employee assigned thereto.

And speaking about "The Extreme Test," it must be noted if only for the record that were it not for these men – Fred Clarke, a white man who made public my letters; three white judges in the Third Circuit Court who rendered judgment; and John Collins, another white man who made public the verdict of The Third Circuit Court as a freelancer for The San Juan Star -- I would never have had the material to write a book telling my readers how I was being persecuted by members of my ethnic group.

Do you remember the irregular behavior of the Virgin Islands National Guard while on duty on the Island of St. Croix during Hurricane Hugo in 1989? The Virgin Islands National Guard deserted the people of St. Croix by running away from their duty in the midst of the storm, and was thereafter (without being charged with desertion) forgiven by Governor Alexander A. Farrelly who, by the way, was ordered by President George H.W. Bush to swear in a new commander appointed by Bush from the United States mainland.

As a people we have made a travesty of the laws of the Virgin Islands. And speaking of Hurricane Hugo and the unacceptable performance of the Virgin Islands National Guard, inevitably it must be noted for the edification of you the reader that in the aftermath of the violent storm a National Guard unit from Washington, D.C. was called in and thereafter assigned the task of providing security for the Crucians which in a sense gave them (the Crucians) freedom from danger and a feeling of being safe. And many thanks to the United States military, who were also on the scene. Because of the military's presence the evacuees were ordered to form lines at the time when food was being served so as to avoid a stampede resulting from a headlong flight of the crowd.

This type of behavior I hasten to add was something in sharp contrast to the days when the standpipe (an auxiliary to a reservoir) was opened, signaling the availability of water from the reservoir for the use of the local people who were without cisterns. Survival of the fittest would always come into play. The strongest man heading for the standpipe would rush thereto with speed and force ready to do battle with anyone daring to engage him, completely oblivious of his fellowman's need for water. There was no way however that the military would allow the strongest man in the crowd to stick his hand in the pot of red peas soup with a view towards getting at the pork. Everybody had to be fed from the pot.

At this juncture, I find it necessary to turn aside from the main subject in order to interject the following: Virgin Islanders have mastered the art of hypocrisy. Through pretentious displays, the local hypocrites continue to sing the praises of Rothschild Francis and Queen Mary (two Virgin Islanders who wore badges of courage), seemingly forgetting that if these two people were alive today displaying the same abrasive attitudes that made them famous, they would be persecuted a la Liston B. Monsanto, Sr., and chastised in words of bitter scorn. This behavioral pattern -- repulsive as it is -- was handed down to the hypocrites by many of our ancestral natives.

Now let us gravitate back to 1931 when President Herbert Hoover on his way back to Washington, D.C., after a visit to St. Thomas stopped briefly in San Juan, Puerto Rico, where in a press conference he described St. Thomas as "An Effective Poorhouse." It was a most veracious description of the Island and, what's more, the local people knew that they had no justification for challenging the veracity of Hoover's statement, but instead of applauding Hoover for having the courage to speak the truth while impulsively opening the door to a transformation of the "Effective Poorhouse" into something more attractive, they lambasted the President, who was a Republican, while denouncing his party. Wouldn't it have been better to agree with Hoover putting him on the defensive by asking him what was going to be done about the "Effective Poorhouse"?

Following that great event, with anger and hatred being emphasized against the Republican Party, given the opportunity to elect a governor for the first time in 1970, many of our people through hypocrisy reconciled with Hoover's Republican Party electing Melvin H. Evans (a Republican) as our first elected governor, thereby causing Cyril E. King, an Independent Citizens Movement candidate who had emerged victorious in the general election, to lose the governorship. Note: although finishing first in the general election, King did not receive the votes needed (50+1) to win the election. As a consequence he was forced into a runoff with Evans.

King was elected governor in November 1974, took the oath of office in January 1975, and died in office in January 1978. The good gentleman, because he was bedridden and incapacitated for several months before his death, hardly had any time as our second elected governor to do anything of consequence except choosing the site for his eponym, i.e., Cyril E. King airport. Yet the local hypocrites continue to sing the praises of a governor who extended the programs of his predecessor, Melvin H. Evans. So here's the logical question. What did Cyril E. King do as our second elected governor that the other elected governors did not do? Admittedly the man had all the earmarks of being a good governor, but unfortunately his tenure of office was shortened by death.

What's alarming about all of this and the other incidents of law-breaking to be explained on the following pages of this book is that, undeniable as the unwritten policy cited at the outset of this chapters is, it has become a well-established principle suitably accepted for such a long period of time that a small group of Virgin Islanders with axes to grind through anti-American sentiments impulsively ignore the local scofflaws while denouncing violently the United States for what they perceive to be the country's failure to respect the treaty between Denmark and the United States as it relates to the acquisition of the Virgin Islands and also the failure of the United States to follow the guidelines established by the United Nations relating to decolonization.

One would think after listening to them that their remarks were intended to be at the least quasi humorous, but in reality these people are very serious. Put simply, what they are saying through intellectual myopia translates into: Virgin Islands history tells us that the Carib Indians are indigenous to the Virgin Islands and American history tells us that the Indians are indigenous to the United States. But whereas the descendants of Africans now own the land previously owned by the Caribs and whereas the descendants of Europeans now own the land previously owned by the Indians, both parties can now brag over the fact that we have something in common, and that is land that previously owned by Indians now belongs to both of us. That point established, we feel safe in saying that we are operating under the principle of laissez-faire, making us free to do as we please. Because of the size of the population of the

United States and the fact that its people are more enlightened than ours, the United States must operate in accordance with the law. Furthermore, unlike the United States, as an unincorporated territory we are trying desperately to eat our cake and still have it. Because we are receiving mixed signals when it comes to our law-breaking ways, which truthfully result in our political candidates being elected to public offices, we do not hesitate in saying to hell with the law, especially as it relates to white-collar crime. As a matter of fact, here in the Virgin Islands where we live, there is no one to check the checker. Finally for your information, it is only when there is a disaster (such as a hurricane) in the Virgin Islands that some people are reminded through FEMA that the Virgin Islands are indeed a territorial possession of the United States.

But back to the more mundane matters of business. Pigeon hearted as our people are when it comes to exposing mismanagement and corruption in government, one would think that after reading "The Extreme Test" they would join me in minimizing what's going on in our government. In the Virgin Islands, like anyplace in the world, there is either a right way or a wrong way. "The Extreme Test" authored by me tells the reader how wrong we are in the Virgin Islands when it comes to carrying out our duties as government employees. What puzzles me is the attitudes of the readers of "The Extreme Test" (many of them no longer on the government's payroll) who are being very emphatic in their desire to impose their ideology on others but inordinately quiet about the wrongdoers who have been exposed in that book. Again I repeat my contention: We are not a sovereign state; consequently, our range is limited with respect to what we can and what we cannot do. Why can't we understand that?

In the other islands in the Caribbean where you do not hear the anti-American sentiments to the degree that you hear them in the United States Virgin Islands, it is clearly understood among the officials at the highest levels in government that the Virgin Islands, because of their status, are prohibited from doing the things that their sovereign states can do. Page 164, paragraph 3, line 11, of my book "Perpetuating the Memory of A Sportscaster" says: "Either we take what's coming to us under our present status as an unincorporated territorial possession of the United States or we ask for our independence from the United States in the same manner that the colonists who colonized New England and the former British colonies in the Caribbean did in getting their independence from England."

What you are about to read was being treated as an idle thought, but after deliberating and finding that it would make a worthwhile paragraph, I decided to include it herewith. Accordingly, here it goes: In the Virgin Islands our major industry is tourism. Mercantile St. Thomas is our chief seaport; hence, the Mecca of our tourism product. Because of their refusal to accept the fact that there is a big difference between service and servitude, 95% of our ancestral natives and native Virgin Islanders combined do not work directly in services, which, we hasten to add, relate directly to tourism. Through false pride, ancestral natives and native Virgin Islanders look down on the service industry, considering it menial since they feel that it's something that lowers their dignity.

Our major hotels and resorts are owned by foreign corporations. Ninety-five percent of the stores in the shopping district are owned by transplants to St. Thomas. The tourist attractions such as The Butterfly Farm, Coral World, The Tramway, and Mahogany Run Golf Course are all owned by foreign corporations. The major supermarkets and filling stations are owned by Arabs. The pharmacies (95 percent of them) are owned by so-called outsiders and 95 percent of the taxicab operators are from the Eastern Caribbean.

Virgin Islanders will continue to find themselves in a quandary over the issue of a change in status. In a referendum dealing with status several years ago, the people (mostly Democrats) voted for the status quo option which translated into "no change." Later on, given the chance to vote in their 2008 Democratic Presidential caucus, the greater number of the same people who had previously voted for the status quo locally voted for candidate Barack H. Obama – a man whose emphasis along his political campaign trail was heavily placed on the word "Change." Yes indeed, in the Virgin Islands we are all for progress unless it involves change.

Honesty is a very provocative thing. Writing the truth as is the case in this book automatically puts you behind the eight ball while turning you into a most despicable person. When it comes to the young men of the Virgin Islands (many of whom are engaging each other in gunfights) the truth must be told. The absence of leadership in government and in many of our households has resulted in the undisciplined society in which we find ourselves. Nobody wants to lead by example.

Never mind the oppressors who are quick to say in strengthening their argument that the same thing is happening globally. Because the Virgin Islands (tiny as they are) are our home, making them number one on our priority list, we must begin the chore of cleaning our houses before worrying about what's happening globally.

Consider carefully the following: After a hard day of work, you head for home, a most hungry person. At home you greet your wife and prepare yourself for a hot plate of fish and fungi. But lo and behold, there is no food. Your wife explains that she has to walk a block away to buy some cornmeal and that her trip to the grocery would take about five minutes or less. She leaves for the grocery and returns to the house about three hours later. When asked what took so long, she explains that on her way to the grocery she ran into an old paramour with whom she made passionate love. She finishes her explanation by saying these kinds of love affairs are taking place globally. It is one that you must accept in the same manner that you've accepted wrong doing globally. Would you accept that? Of course not. Here's hoping that you get the point of the story.

You may recall that in Chapter I of this book, I extracted an excerpt from the holier than thou address given by Governor Alexander A. Farrelly before the Virgin Islands Legislature on January 16, 1987. That the address was a grandstand play that would eventually turn Farrelly's halo into a noose around his neck surfaced when he failed to legally bring formal charges against any of the nameless people whom he had accused of being in violation of law. What Alexander Farrelly stood for on January 16th, 1987, would not be legally practiced by his administration. Following his address, he immediately joined forces with a merry throng of scofflaws.

A bird's eye view into his law-breaking activities would disclose that the good governor had a propensity for confusing sentiment with justice. He became a delinquent taxpayer and thereafter lied to the public when he said that the delinquency had been satisfied. (See page 398, paragraphs six and seven of "The Extreme Test"). Given the choice in defense of his signing a questionable contract, he chose (through willing obedience), in a paraphrase, "I signed the contract even though I did not read it in detail" over "I read and signed the contract." To the employees' consternation, he gave his approval to his pitiless lieutenants in the Virgin Islands Bureau of Internal Revenue to keep down unjustly and by cruelty many of the employees who were free from sin and wrong. Let's face it, there was nothing even remotely resembling a change of attitude between Farrelly and his predecessors.

In the Virgin Islands, sadly to say, anything dealing with truth is (as they say in England) sent to Coventry. Disregarding commonly accepted rules and principles is nothing new. It all started in 1970 with the advent of the elected governor. The local Democratic Party's political dominance (hegemony) took over. For starters they formed an unholy alliance with the Republican Party helping them to elect Melvin H. Evans as our first elected governor. For your information, it has become almost a mantra for the scofflaws to say we do things the Virgin Islands way.

Scofflaws believe that they have an overriding responsibility to break the law. Too often we have heard of cars being legally parked and too often we have heard about these cars being blocked in so as to prevent the legally parked car from moving in any direction. It matters not to the illegally parked driver that he's in violation of law. Like a bride bedecked with her jewels, he strolls to his car (long on brawn and short on brains) ready for an argument. He doesn't care one whit about the legally parked car. And then there are those who literally take the right of way from you. They come out of intersections with reckless abandon, forcing you to yield to their demands.

Although unique as individuals, collectively we are hypocritical and proud enough to point out that crime is a global problem and that the Virgin Islands have not been granted immunity from global problems. This approach is the general tendency among the scofflaws. The people of the Virgin Islands continue to adopt the bad things that are taking place globally because presumably there are no good things happening worldwide that's worthwhile.

A comparative analysis of New York City and the Virgin Islands when it comes to power outages would reveal that whereas (for the purpose of this comparison), New York experiences a power outage every fifty years, if ever, in the Virgin Islands – a much smaller land mass – we have power outages every three days. Operating on the thesis that silence is golden, the people's silence on power outages is a matter that remains deafening. And now that you have received my message that I'm not good at quibbling, I ask that you bear with me once more as I bring your attention back to The Scofflaws.

Above and beyond what you have just read are a group of unlicensed taxicab drivers hereinafter referred to as gypsy taxicab drivers and/or gypsies. In the Virgin Islands and St. Thomas proper, gypsy taxicab drivers cruise for fares even though they are licensed as privately owned. These drivers needless to say cannot qualify for the type of insurance needed to taxi passengers from place to place. What's more, they do not contribute to the treasury of the Virgin Islands. Put simply, they do not pay taxes on their income.

Most of our gypsy taxicab drivers are immigrants (some naturalized, the status of others unknown) from the foreign islands in the eastern Caribbean, making it safe to say that St. Thomas is the transshipment point from where they ship their ill-gotten gains back to their homelands. They have become a most ubiquitous bunch. Gypsy taxicab drivers have been given the key to the island of St. Thomas by the duly licensed taxicab drivers. At a time when the government of the Virgin Islands is in desperate straits for money you'd think that the taxicab drivers allowed by law would take umbrage with a view towards filing an application to a court for justice.

Because it is an incendiary issue and one that may result in the defeat of many of our public officials at the polls, no one would dare tell the gypsy taxicab drivers (who have become victims of delusion) that they must discontinue the illegal practice. It is an undeniable fact that everyone in a position of authority is enamored with these scofflaws.

Persecuted and ostracized by a cadre of miscreants and lawless government officials for of all things working in accordance with established guidelines, I was forced to operate a licensed taxicab from where I could impart my knowledge of the Virgin Islands to my passengers. Knowing that during the period of my persecution that the governors of the Virgin Islands were governing by osmosis and being wary of what was going on in the business of which I had become a part, I (at times) watched surreptitiously as the gypsies plied their illegal activity. I was fully aware of the fact that in the Virgin Islands when the law is enforced against scofflaws it produces a negative attitude towards the enforcement agent and results in a vote against the administration. But, having said that, I must add that I was also aware of the common belief that law enforcement is very important to the success of an administration. Be that as it may, finding myself immersed in the culture of the Virgin Islands and knowing that I had become a victim of the same government that was allowing the gypsies to operate in violation of law, I thought it an opportune moment to write an open letter to the local Daily News of December 15th, 1993, which said:

The Daily News, Wednesday, December 15, 1993

Letters

Are gypsies above the law?

Dear editor:

Recent events have brought about an undercurrent of sadness in the laughter of many of our local taxi drivers. They find themselves hemmed in — victims of aggression.

The foregoing serves as my introduction. Now in order to arrive at the essential part of my editorial, let me begin my saying that voluntary compliance is the keystone to our whole Virgin Islands tax structure.

In order to do what is lawful, most people in the Virgin Islands voluntarily disclose their taxable activities by filing a return without notice and paying the tax due.

To maintain and strengthen our voluntary compliance system for the purpose of corralling that small group of people who are not now complying with what the laws prescribe, efforts are often made to educate with an eye toward enforcing — in the hope that such enforcement action would force obedience.

In The Daily News, Dec. 6, there appears — under the heading of "Business briefs," a hidden message which in a paraphrase calls upon duly licensed taxi drivers to make a vicarious sacrifice for unlicensed taxi drivers (aka gypsies) who pride themselves on impersonating taxi drivers.

In earnest, taxi drivers (who it seems have no protection under the law) are being reminded to make sure they get a tax clearance letter from the Virgin Islands Bureau of Internal Revenue before trying to renew their business licenses. No notification is given to the "gypsy taxi drivers," however. With them, it's business as usual.

But in-as-much-as it has been established that most people in the Virgin Islands feel security and safety in numbers take precedence over lawfulness. The governor's failure to protect the taxi drivers against the impersonators may well result in taxi drivers discarding their licenses and registrations for the sole purpose of becoming "gypsies," thereby circumventing the law and authorities of the Virgin Islands.

Man's inhumanity to man continues to wreak havoc on taxi drivers. They have been placed in a most untenable position by a Virgin Islands government who has given them permission to operate through the issuance of valid licenses, while simultaneously allowing "gypsies" to operate in violation of law.

Liston B. Monsanto

St. Thomas

(Note: The Daily News misprinted my letter. The 7th paragraph should have read "But in as much as it has been established that most people in the Virgin Islands feel security and safety in numbers take precedence over lawfulness, the governor's failure to protect the taxi drivers against the impersonators may well result in taxi drivers discarding their licenses and registrations for the sole purpose of becoming "gypsies," thereby circumventing the law and authorities of the Virgin Islands.)

Then, adhering to established customs and traditions, Mr. Silvio Soto took liberty of action to address an ill-advised letter to The Daily News of December 20, 1993, which said:

Gypsies are filling a void

Dear editor:

Permit me to reply to the letter that was carried in your Dec. 15 edition entitled: "Are gypsies above the Law?"

A simple study of gypsies would prove that they are providing a service that regular taxi drivers do not.

During a 24-hour period (per day), you will find gypsies only at the supermarkets, in the streets and at late night clubs. Without gypsy service, locals would be stranded in the streets, waiting for a taxi.

The gypsies are not at the cruise ship docks, beaches, airport or at the local taxi stands.

The question stands, "Where are the taxi drivers at night?"

You would find them parked at Nelson Mandela Circle from 9 p.m. to 5 a.m. waiting to go in the taxi line at West Indian Co. dock, or at the airport taxi stand from 5 a.m. to wait for the big jets that arrive from the United States after 12 a.m.

Mr. Monsanto, as far as I am concerned, it is the private tour operators and the hotels that offer transportation to their guests to various locations on the island, which are hurting the V.I. taxi drivers, not the gypsy drivers.

Silvio Soto
St. Thomas

Prejudice had warped Mr. Soto's judgment. He had become a little bit more than disingenuous with his remarks. And so once again, after labeling his letter barnyard waste, I issued a reply through The Daily News of January 6, 1994.

Gypsy debate continues

Dear editor:

Throw an object (an old shoe for example) in a pack of dogs and you are guaranteed that the one that gets hit hollers.

Silvio Soto's letter (Dec. 20) on behalf of a bunch of law-breaking gypsy taxi drivers is not responsive to my letter which appeared in your newspaper of Dec. 15. He completely missed the point. So hard was he hit by the old shoe, he reacted without thinking.

Judging from the contents of his letter, it doesn't matter to him that gypsies are filling a void in violation of law, nor does it matter to him that a government devoid of taxes is useless.

The gentlemen is so full of energy that he cannot keep still.

Maybe he ought to spend some of his time on some worthwhile reading on what's allowed by law. It would be a delight were he to channel all his efforts into a project designed to legitimize gypsies. I rest my case.

Liston Monsanto
St. Thomas

Knowing that only a callous person can see suffering without trying to relieve it, a Mr. Warren F. Bowers, of the belief that the gypsy taxicab drivers were suffering from my attack and acting as a voluntary agent for Mr. Soto and the gypsies, wrote to The Daily News of January 12th, 1994, in this fashion:

In defense of gypsy taxis

Dear editor:

I do not necessarily condone the gypsy taxi operators, but at least they will pick up and deliver local residents, at reasonable rates. They pay highway taxes on vehicles that they purchase and probably pay as much personal income tax as other taxi operators. The other taxi operators would rather gouge the visitors than pick up locals.

A recent letter from Mr. (Liston) Monsanto talks about the legality of the gypsy operators. At Cyril E. King Airport, the rates to various destinations are posted with the per passenger charge. Recently at 7:30 p.m. on a Saturday night, the dispatcher and driver demanded a fee of $45 to take a party of three to Sugar Bay Plantation. They stated that the passengers could either pay that amount or wait until the van was full.

Warner F. Bowers
St. Thomas

Because I had already rested my case in my letter of January 6th, 1994, and because I could find no good reason to write to Mr. Bowers and Mr. Soto who were now collaborating with a bunch of scofflaws in violation of existing law, I thought it wise to leave them alone with their law-breaking ways. Four years later, I was forced to write once again to The Daily News of March 25, 1998, after the subject of gypsy taxicab drivers had been brought back into the news. My letter said:

Letters

Just enforce existing laws

Dear editor:

While some of our inhabitants (without general knowledge of the subject) continue to cheer with abandon, gypsy taxi drivers are again back in the news.

Why? Because they are the only laid-back methodical unlicensed group whose vocation operates ubiquitously and free of taxation.

And amid this showy display our governor finds himself worried over the earned-income tax credit, which — to put in a paraphrase — is an unfunded mandate that is serving only to cripple the territory's finances.

The serendipity of the two newsworthy but separate pieces of information (earned income and tax-exempted gypsy taxi drivers) seems too good to be true.

Consequently, I feel constrained to write hoping that the people in whom the authority is vested would understand the nature and gravity of the problems, and that those who have the power to act — at all levels of government — would listen and respond.

Lest we forget, no one is justified in doing evil on the grounds of expediency and if scofflaws are ignored and allowed to play their illicit trade ostentatiously before the public (i.e. disregarding rules, etc.) it can be predicted as a certainty that they will begin begetting more scofflaws.

And so if the powers-that-be are not impervious to suggestions, I'd like to recommend we enforce existing laws instead of trying to exercise the function of legislation intended to appease or otherwise legalize the culprits and simultaneously create replacements.

The enforcement of existing laws would easily dispose of the regulars while preventing others from engaging in the same illegal practice.

Liston B. Monsanto
St. Thomas

The gypsy taxicab matter had become a source of annoyance. Owing to the government's failure to enforce the law, I found myself (in the interest of being consistent) writing letters to The Daily News in a vain attempt to reach a host of law-breaking gypsies who like many people in the Virgin Islands do not read The Daily News regularly. About sixteen months following my letter of March 25, 1998, I wrote another letter dated July 12, 1999, repeating my contention to the scofflaws and the many government officials who, unlike the gypsies, presumably read it. Here is what that letter said:

The Daily News, Monday, July 12, 1999

▼ Letters

Go home gypsy

Dear editor:

Nowadays in the Virgin Islands the pageantry of law breaking has become a spectacular display. The daunting task of ridding the islands of an illegal gypsy taxi operation is a classic example.

Because the Virgin Islands Government has not been strict with the enforcement of the laws by which taxi cabs, etc., operate, an inversion of justice is presently being perpetrated upon the people of the Virgin Islands. And it is either by intention or through ignorance that many people are publicly paying reverence and speaking out with great fervor glorifying a select group of gypsy taxi drivers who continue to operate in violation of the law.

Gypsy taxi drivers and all their ilk (e.g., our local brothels and drug dealers who are all filling a void and providing much-needed services) have become an endemic disease occurring in several forms and characterized by general apathy on the part of our government.

The time has come to show those who regularly flout the law that their ingenuity does not exceed those of the law enforcement agencies.

Those in positions of authority must "do what is right for it will gratify some people and astonish the rest."

For bonafide taxpayers to promote and/or otherwise sing the praises of the gypsy taxi driver and others who are not filling and paying their fair share of taxes is disgraceful.

Registered taxis whose medallions have been devalued because of the gypsies must be forced to form line at the various places now being illegally served by the gypsies. Lest we forget, the registered taxis were issued licenses by the Virgin Islands Government to serve the public in a manner reflective of their modus operandi at the hotels, the West Indian Company Dock, and the airport.

Liston B. Monsanto. Sr.
St. Thomas

Based on the contents of my letters, one can readily see that the gypsies have a legion of supporters. In my quest to solicit the assistance of my fellow taxicab drivers (at random) I found that they too welcomed the illegal activity. Why? Because they had no desire to taxi the local people. Anyway, on August 2, 1999, once again to The Daily News I wrote:

The Daily News, August 2, 1999

Letters

Gypsy-taxi drivers

Dear editor:

Today, forced by circumstances and utter exasperation and with an aura of distress riding among a group of registered taxi drivers, I feel duty-bound to write (once again) about our influential, law-breaking "gypsy-taxi drivers!"

Because I'm not enamored about the licentiousness, and because I know that some people in positions of authority within the Virgin Islands governmental structure have difficulty in separating truth from falsehood and fact from fiction, and furthermore, because I know that many of these people do not read very fast, I've decided to write this letter very slowly hoping to make them understand that you do not reward people for doing what is wrong. You punish them.

For proof, you may ask any person convicted by a court or, better yet, any person (David Eddie comes to mind) presently serving a prison sentence.

With all the criminal activity in the Virgin Islands (most of which have been brought about by licentiousness) and with most of our senators calling for compulsory automobile insurance, who among these same senators would be so bereft of his senses that he'd consider rewarding wrong by way of legislation? Old habits undoubtedly die hard.

Ponder this: An enterprising merchant without a valid Virgin Islands license decides to set up shop directly outside a Main Street store peddling the same wares as that store. Would he be issued a "Class B license" for forgoing an alliance with that store? Gentlemen, please do not allow your fears to cloud your judgment. Enough is as good as a feast. Please spare us the histrionics.

There is a fairly simple way to avoid the vexing problem of "gypsy-taxi drivers." Law enforcement! Need I say more?

Liston Monsanto Sr.
St. Thomas

And there is more. August 18, 1999, I wrote the following:

The Daily News, Wednesday, August 18, 1999

▼

Letters

Breakdown in justice

Dear editor:

First off, for the edification and upliftment of the reader, the following quotation coming from the prolific writer Thomas Jefferson is being used as a preface to this letter: "The most valuable of all talents is that of never using two words when one will do."

As the proud owner of a taxi medallion, I've spoken ad nauseam about a Virgin Islands government which continues to operate on the thesis that due largely to extenuating circumstances, one cannot practice law by the book at any time.

As I write, the contentious issue of taxicabs (duly registered and gypsies) has made for good fodder on many radio talk shows locally. That it has become a subject of poignant interest is a massive understatement.

The callers sadden and anger me. Many of them influenced more by impulse than by reason continue to reason cleverly but falsely, especially in regard to right or wrong. This behavior --

presumably accepted by the public, transcends disbelief and consequently has left me in a state of wonderment.

And so today it is without a lot of explanation and commentary, that I feel safe in saying that in spite of diversions intended to cloud the issue, the Virgin Islands government -- a government whose history is replete with memorable moments, has become blameworthy. Their principle of letting people do as they please continues to engender violence.

The duly registered cabs and the gypsies are both taking advantage of an opportunity given to them by the Virgin Islands government.

Public hearings and legislation are not the answer. Law enforcement is: To reward lawbreakers as posing as pioneers for their law-breaking ways, will result only in other lawbreakers doing the same thing for which their predecessors were rewarded.

Liston B. Monsanto Sr.
St. Thomas

Then on October 27, 1999, I delivered the following letter to The Daily News:

The Daily News, October 27, 1999

Letters

On gypsy taxis

Dear editor:

Several months ago in defense of my taxi medallion, I assumed the role of "persuasive agent for positive change" and immediately thereafter I made the decision between duly registered taxi drivers and an elite group of law-breaking drivers masquerading under the guise of gypsy taxis.

Because I dared to speak the truth about what I considered to be a troublesome invasion by the gypsies into the affairs of the legitimate taxi drivers, a great many of my detractors, who incidentally are too tough to be honest and too weak to lead, joined with the Philistines and Toadies of the Virgin Islands and together they wrote me off.

Instead of taking the time to review and consider the points made in my letters, they — while hobnobbing and brainstorming at the various "nerve centers" around the island —made light of the matter and verbally attacked me placing emphasis on, of all things, my choice of words.

But while these people treated my letters as something of little importance, the villainous government's reaction demonstrated that they (the letters) had a tremendous impact.

At a time when the Virgin Islands government is desperately in need of money, those in positions of authority could no longer sidestep or ignore the issue. Today their actions are speaking much louder than their words.

Due largely to my letters, things are being brought to a head. One does not have to be soft on crime, a bleeding heart or even a member of the taxi cab organization to detect the undercurrent of animosity and frustration

So other than the subject matter being a good chapter for a book, I feel safe in saying that the Virgin Islands government is making positive inroads into the gypsy taxi dilemma.

Now it can be predicted as a certainty that tomorrow will be a decidedly better day than today. Hats off to the new administration. It's an undeniable, but true, fact of life that "success comes from hanging on when everyone else has let go."

Liston B. Monsanto Sr.
St. Thomas

Do we have a problem with the gypsy taxicab drivers? The answer is yes. They are tax evaders who must be made to file and pay their taxes in the same manner that Al Capone the racketeer finally did. Is the Virgin Islands Government -- a government operating in violation of law -- willing to perform its duty of law enforcement? Maybe. I'll say this much, however. If an alternative in violation of law (not favorable to the gypsies) is found, it's going to be very costly to any governor wishing to be re-elected. And let me tell you, folks; that's a risk that no incumbent governor is willing to take.

Back to scofflaws and their law-breaking ways. Perhaps what should be considered a dramatic performance because of its prominence and the fact that it has resurrected an old custom is the altercation between Mr. Louis M. Willis (currently executive director of the Virgin Islands Legislature) and Senator Adlah "Foncie" Donastorg, Jr., which took place on the premises of the capitol building on October 14th, 2009.

At the Virgin Islands Bureau of Internal Revenue where Mr. Willis worked before becoming executive director of the Virgin Islands Legislature, he was given full authority as a hireling without interest or pride in his work. He was guided by influential wrongdoers who instructed him to use the rule of thumb in arbitrarily carrying out the duties of his office. For this reason, Mr. Willis became swell headed, excessively proud, and contemptuous toward his fellow men.

As members of the world of scholars and government officials in positions of authority, Governor Alexander A. Farrelly -- a man whose name is enshrined in the building housing the Alexander A. Farrelly Justice Center -- Mr. Anthony P. Olive, and Mr. Edward E. Thomas (two former directors of the Virgin Islands Bureau of Internal Revenue) were given a convenient occasion through the usage of their college degrees to discipline Mr. Willis for overtly displaying his irresistible and abnormal desire for fighting in the workplace.

Starting in May of 1988 and continuing up to November of 1992, when I officially retired from government, Farrelly, Olive, and Thomas were told in writing -- by me (see "The Extreme Test") -- about Mr. Willis' behavior on several occasions. Needless to say, my letters were ignored. Their taste for law and order was perverted only because the complaints were coming from Liston Monsanto. Had these good for nothings inflicted some form of punishment on Mr. Willis after receiving my letters, chances are what happened on October 14th, 2009, surrounding the altercation between Willis and Donastorg would never have taken place.

And now, in order to make this chapter complete, I offer for your reading pleasure the following article written by me to The Daily News of April 23rd, 1993. It makes for good reading.

Reaping what government sows

Liston Monsanto is a retired V.I. government worker.

Liston Monsanto

Guest Editorial

Because they have the ability to couch their ideas and feelings in beautiful language, here in the U.S. Virgin Islands and St. Thomas proper the wrongdoers in government — working with the assistance of certain members of the press —continue to be an elusive enemy.

They've been operating contrary to law for so long that even though they know that our political system causes much damage, they cannot help but favor reaction. Indentured to the system they take great comfort in knowing that they can attack the so-called ordinary people.

All of a sudden they have forgotten that taxicab operators — licensed by the Virgin Islands government — are an integral part of an undisciplined Virgin Islands society.

The wrongdoers firmly believe that they are accountable but not culpable for the transgressions of taxicab operators, who have been made to conform to the norms and mores of the same Virgin Islands society whose government has issued them licenses to operate their vehicles.

While the activities of the taxicab operators continue to be monitored and their performances evaluated by a motley group of reviewers (tourists from the real world) whose standards and outlook on life are far different from ours, taxicab operators in the Virgin Islands who can do no more than reflect the environment in which they were trained are being told by their detractors (with tongue in cheek of course) that clean up their act they must. Incidentally, I wonder how the wrongdoers would fare after being evaluated by these same reviewers.

I have become so bewildered over the wrongdoers' call for changed attitudes and the implementation of stern measures or swift disciplinary action against the taxi cab operators, that I feel duty bound to let them know that to undertake a project relating to a change in attitudes would be contingent upon a change in the unbusiness-like approach they have chosen to aid them in carrying out their duties. Lest we forget, there can be no growth without change.

Following Hurricane Hugo whispering hope became the order of the day among the wrongdoers, who were desperately hoping for everything to remain status quo. That their hopes ended in fruition is really an understatement.

A change from the status quo would have caused widespread distress. Taxicab operators and everybody else would have started life anew with changed attitudes.

But now that it has become abundantly clear that the wrongdoers' cries for changed attitudes are more symbolic than tangible, I find it most appropriate to use the following quotation: "Those who corrupt the public's mind are just as evil as those who steal from the public's purse."

Mark well my words.

CHAPTER III

BEWILDERED PEOPLE

With respect to the crime wave that's currently moving through the Virgin Islands and St. Thomas proper, I feel constrained to say for your spiritual benefit that with the advent of the elected governor in 1970 the decadence of morals became a major factor in our manner of living.

Politicians seeking to be elected to the various offices with the assistance of their supporting cast began showing utter disregard for the law. Through platitudes from glib tongues they became politically correct and highly immoral.

Unlike a whole lot of uneducated parents and guardians of the period, the politicians serving as the vanguard for others of their ilk (some enjoying academic lives) knew that the home, school, and church were the chief formative influences in a child's life. Many of them also knew that in the decades of the '30s and '40s the children attending the various elementary public schools were legally required to attend their respective church every Wednesday afternoon at three o'clock for classes in religious instructions while at the same time completing the circuit of home, school, and church. Today in St. Thomas (unlike the '30s and '40s) per capita we have more churches than any place under the American flag. This being the case, we should not have any problems with our children going to church on a regular basis nor, I hasten to add, should we have a problem with prayer in school.

Before digesting or rebuking what was just mentioned above, I suggest you take a cursory glance at many of the churches' rituals which undoubtedly would reveal that a great number of the various officers in the church are the same ones playing key roles in the state. Needless to say the motives for their actions are insincere and selfish.

With social natures (partying every day), the people of the Virgin Islands have proven time after time that man is indeed a social being. Obligated to a totalitarian governmental system which demands mediocrity we have made our islands fit for living with so-called outsiders who are taking full advantage of a people loaded with abysmal ignorance.

The people making up our establishment together with our politicians don't give a whit about unqualified people being placed in positions of authority. Their only concern sadly to say is being voted into office by these people who as if you did not know make up the mass of mankind locally. And because of the environment in which they find themselves, underachievers, unlettered people, many of our "Ancestral Native Virgin Islanders" and "Native Virgin Islanders" as defined by the delegates making up the Fifth Constitutional Convention are without self-love, self-respect, and self-discipline. As naysayers bound by political patronage they continue to be in denial of many of the wrongs in the Virgin Islands. They have failed to see that unlike the rank of a king or queen whose followers are glued to them through rigid adherence the people in positions of authority are not endowed with royal power. Moreover, they continue to see a group of people whose members are considered possible replacements in the line of succession for the various governors and finally they do not entertain the thought that their children (one day) with the proper training and education can rise to the top of the heap becoming governors of the Virgin Islands.

As concerns the local politicians they take tremendous pride in dishing out a form of political science called "Low Root" locally and exploit with joy the disadvantaged voters of the Virgin Islands.

They are always quick with ready answers relative to their version of things knowing full well that a people suffering from political ineptitude would be gullible enough to accept them. Sometimes as humans they may make a slip in speech, conduct, or manners, but certain members of the press are always there standing ready in damage control mode with red herrings and innocuous questions trying desperately to clean up the image of the politicians. The same thing holds true when it comes to the many people in positions of authority throughout the Virgin Islands Government. Quid pro quo is the name of the game which officially began in 1970 with the advent of the elected governor. Again I ask that you read "The Extreme Test," a book which sheds a lot of light on the great restrictions placed upon the freedom of individuals who dared to speak out about the illegal practices at the Virgin Islands Bureau of Internal Revenue.

A classic example of the press operating incognito with a view towards protecting liars and law-breakers appears in an article written in "Pride Magazine" featuring Anthony P. Olive.

Anthony P. Olive became a perfunctory director of the then Tax Division sometime in 1975 under Commissioner of Finance Leroy A. Quinn. When the Bureau of Internal Revenue was created Olive was demoted to a position of figurehead under Quinn who became the Bureau's director. Following Quinn's departure he moved up to the positions of perfunctory director and whipping boy for Governor Alexander A. Farrelly under the leadership of director de facto Edward E. Thomas. Finally, his days of playing the role of Fakir (a Muslim holy man who lives by begging) came to an end with Farrelly's appointment of Edward Thomas as the new director of the Bureau. Farrelly immediately shipped Olive into exile to sit in a corner (away from his career occupation) at the Department of Commerce from where he would retire ultimately.

Now when you contrast birds with fishes you can see their differences. So too when you compare what I've written above to what you are about to read in the following article from "Pride Magazine."

ANTHONY OLIVE

AS ISLANDS FACE CRISIS, SPOTLIGHT TURNS ON OLIVE

The Virgin Islands Bureau of Internal Revenue has a staff of slightly more than 100, considerably smaller than several of the major departments. but it stands near the top in importance because of the vital role it plays in collecting most of the revenue which the Virgin Islands Government needs to finance its varied operations. The critical importance of the V.I. Internal Revenue Bureau is appreciated much more these days when officials scramble after every dollar available to erase a deficit of nearly $30 million before the fiscal year closes on September 30.

Annually the tax collection agency raises approximately $100,000,000 in individual income tax payments. Another $28 million is collected from corporations. Gross receipts and trade and excise taxes yield another $35 million. Thus the Bureau collects about $163 million of the $250 million that the Virgin Islands Government spends annually.

The Internal Revenue Bureau was established a few years ago, after Federal officials threatened to take over the tax collection functions of the territory. In effect, the Tax Division of the Department of Finance became the IRB, but with its own independent director and power to adopt its own policies.

Indicative of the importance of the agency was the decision of the Commissioner of Finance, the late Leroy Quinn, to "step down" from the commissionership to take the directorship of the Internal Revenue Bureau. Moving with Quinn was Anthony Olive, who was then director of the Tax Bureau. He became Quinn's assistant in the new agency. When Quinn resigned eighteen months ago Olive was elevated to the top job.

He is in the spotlight as the Governor and Senators struggle over the huge deficit and debate the catastrophic alternatives to raising funds to .wipe it out. A reduction of the work week for government employees, elimination of several paid holidays, and even the dismissal of large numbers of workers have been discussed.

Olive has given counsel to Governor Juan Luis

as he prepared recommendations to deal with the fiscal crisis, but he has also appeared on numerous occasions before the Legislature to answer questions and to defend his and the administration's recommendations. He has been articulate and forceful.

In the final analysis, the degree to which the Virgin Islands Government regains fiscal health will depend very heavily on the efforts of Mr. Olive and his staff in the Bureau of Internal Revenue.

The volume of work for the small number of persons on the IRB appears overwhelming. He estimates 45,000 to 50,000 individual returns are filed annually, and the returns have been increasing steadily over the last few years. 50% of the returns come from low-income individuals, while 35 % are filed by the middle-income group. High income taxpayers account for the remainder.

Olive warned that a little noticed earned income credit provision in the tax code cost the Virgin Islands Government $2 million this year, and undoubtedly the cost will go up. If a wage earner earns $5,000 or less a year and has a dependent child he can claim a $500 payment upon filing of his tax return. Under President Reagan's new tax proposal that credit will rise to $700, thus imposing new burdens on the local treasury.

Of course, many self-employed residents of the Virgin Islands have refused to file income tax returns, and Olive warned that they are hurting themselves and their dependents as a result. If many of those who are self-employed file and pay the tax due, they become eligible for social security benefits which could be substantial when they reach retirement age or become disabled. And the benefits are passed on to their dependents. When they fail to qualify for social security benefits and find themselves in need of assistance, the burden falls on the local government and its limited resources, Director Olive pointed out.

He believes that the problem of tax evasion is no greater in the territory than on the mainland, but with an increase in staff and the assignment of special agents the Bureau is mounting a campaign to snare evaders and cheats. Three individuals who recently retired from the U.S. Internal Revenue Service have been employed, "our own people have been trained, and we are going after more returns and will audit larger returns," Mr. Olive declared. He pridefully pointed out that while the gross taxes in the United States have fallen due to lower rates, individual tax collections in the territory continue to improve because of improved enforcement and larger audits.

APPEALS TO BUSINESS COMMUNITY

Director Olive estimates that $5million could be collected almost immediately if there is cooperation in the business community. All they have to do is to remit taxes withheld from employees on a timely basis, he emphasized. He said the law requires up to $500 in withheld taxes to be remitted by the end of the quarter. If the withholding is more than $500 and up to $3,000, it must be sent to the Bureau by the 15th day of the succeeding month. But if the withholding taxes are over $3000 the employer is required to remit payments to the Bureau every third day.

Olive said there are substantial penalties for failure to comply with the law and regulations, and he urged voluntary compliance by the business community. If we obtain that cooperation, the fiscal crisis would not be as bad as it is, he in-

7

Liston Monsanto, Sr.

Pride Magazine (cont.)

sisted.

Several cases involving suspected fraud have been referred to the Bureau's Criminal Intelligence Unit. These special investigations will increase since, for the first time, the Bureau has two special agents who specialize in fraud cases. For four and a half years, the Bureau had only one special agent. Olive revealed that for the first time in recent years a native Virgin Islander has been appointed and trained as a special agent, and he is currently working under the direction and leadership of a retired special agent. Reports we have received indicate the need for at least one more special agent, he said, and he vowed to give special priority to that matter as soon as additional funds are received.

Lack of adequate equipment is one of Director Olive's biggest problems. "We have one typewriter that is 18 years old.' He insisted that it is impossible to get maximum production from employees who do not have the necessary tools to do the job.

Training programs for employees at all levels were termed a high priority. We have a very good relation with the U.S. Internal Revenue Service, and we are welcome to send our staff members to the IRS training center in Atlanta, Georgia, but right now we lack the funds to take advantage of those training programs, Olive disclosed.

Despite the handicaps, Olive says his agents are reaching more taxpayers, and delinquent accounts are being reduced. He had special commendation for Jerome Ferdinand, who handles the St. Croix accounts for making significant progress with old accounts. The St. Thomas division, under Kenneth Hansen, has expanded and we are now attacking all of our large accounts, the Director stated.

There is satisfactory coordination between the headquarters in St. Thomas and the St. Croix operations, which are headed by Graciano Belardo. And Mr. Olive singled out Edward Thomas for special praise. There is no assistant to the Director because the job is in the unclassified service and therefore unattractive to the one or two persons who would qualify for it. But Mr. Thomas fills in by currently wearing three hats—serving as head reviewer, classifier and supervising the work of agents to make sure that all cases are handled in accordance with the correct procedures. The work load for Thomas is so great I have to give him some help soon, Olive promised.

Olive himself has been working 15 hours a day for many months, not only handling the significantly increased work load of the Bureau, but responding to numerous requests from the Governor and Senators for information which they believe will be helpful to them as they wrestled with the territory's financial problem. Recently, he said he obtained some relief when he hired Anthony Attidore to assist in handling personnel and budgetary matters within the department.

Olive said he is against halting the payment of refunds to enable the government to balance its budget. Refunds processed during the current fiscal year totaled almost 21,000, more than half representing refunds due in fiscal year 1984. "We are still making payments, but with the present financial crisis, there may come a time when we exhaust the refund reserve." $12 million has been paid out in refunds this year. Olive said that many taxpayers overpay in withholding taxes to save money for summer vacations and other personal needs.

Next August will mark the 21st anniversary of Olive's relationship with the Department of Finance and its offshoot, the IRB. He moved up rapidly , advancing from Revenue Agent I to III over a six-year period. He always took advantage of training courses conducted by the U.S. Internal Revenue Service. From Group Supervisor he was appointed to the position of director of the then Tax Division in the Dept. of Finance. He held that post for four years until the Bureau was established in August 1980. By the end of the year he was named Deputy Director.

Even while he took advanced management courses provided by the IRS, Olive studied in the Master's program of the College of the Virgin Islands, and on May 26 he was awarded a Master's degree in Business Administration.

A graduate of Sts. Peter and Paul High School, class of 1960, he earned his B.A. at St.Bernard College, Cullman, Alabama in 1965. He won the Wall Street Journal Student Achievement Award and was vice president of Pi Gamma Mu, the National Social Science Honor Society. He was listed in Who's Who among students in American universities and colleges.

Mr. Olive's wife, Cecilia, has been employed at First Pennsylvania Bank for the past 24 years, and last April was named Senior Banking Officer.

Tony and Cecilia Olive have two children. Stephanie graduated from Sts.Peter and Paul in 1984 with high honors and has completed one year at Oxford College of Emory University,Atlanta. She is enrolled in the pre-Med program.

Stephens graduated in June from Sts. Peter and Paul with highest honors, and he will attend Oxford College to study Lab Technology.

Fishing, softball and baseball are Mr. Olive's principal hobbies—when he can find the time to devote to them.

As a supervisor at any level in the Virgin Islands government, Anthony P. Olive was useless and inefficient.

Through relentless invective and a holier than thou attitude while on air, Lee Carle has been severely critical of Judge Leon Kendall -- a judge who has yet to be charged with official misconduct for exercising his discretionary power.

When the Williams Family took out a half-page ad in the local Daily News critical of Lee, he was thereafter glorified as a hero via several testimonials. At his testimonial tacitly they were saying members of the Williams family are trying to change things. The man's human and lest you forget, to err is human. What's important is that Lee Carle knows the Island and its disadvantaged people. And that makes him our man at the helm of the damage control wheel. Our advantages with him as our damage control specialist far outweigh any of our disadvantages. Here now for your reading pleasure is the ad taken out by the Williams Family.

All Virgin Islanders Interested in Truth and Justice

On Thursday, February 5, 1998, a member of my family, who is a student at the Charlotte Amalie High School was senselessly shot by a peer. As a result of this disturbing incident, family members are faced with having to deal with the reality of this violent act for the rest of our lives in addition to defending our principles that have been questioned as a result of Lee Carl's report "A Drug Deal Gone Bad."

Does he realize the ramifications of his reporting of misleading and often times false information? This media personality, Lee Carl, has over the years reported to the public erroneous information obtained from that "so call" reliable and sometimes unidentified source, without proper research to obtain the pertinent facts. Did Lee Carl consider providing the information that he received to the proper authorities for investigation before he made this information public? Does he know who are the family of the injured student and how their lives would be affected? Apparently, he did not take the time to weigh any of these factors. However, he continues to report unsubstantiated stories. He himself announced that his report was not based on information from the police investigation.

Lee Carl over the years has short changed this community in his news break-ins. Not too long ago, he announced an incident that took place at BCB Jr. High when it actually occurred at Ivanna Eudora Kean High School, and he even reported that a student involved was deceased. He announced the demise of former governor Juan Luis, which was obtained from a reliable source. Additionally, he most recently reported a robbery at Chase Manhattan Bank that never occurred–to mention the fire at Island Laundries. When will we stand up against this non-investigative reporting? This is my stance on behalf of the Williams family. Rumors have a way of escalating in these islands and even more so with the unprofessional reporting of Lee Carl, for his communication reaches the ears of thousands of Virgin Islanders.

Hopefully, Virgin Islanders have realized that Lee Carl reports tend to be unreliable and we have the common sense to wait until investigative facts are reported before making assumptions or arriving at conclusions. The question is... what institution did Mr. Lee Carl attend for journalist studies? For it is apparent that he needs a refresher course or two, it is the responsibility of all those that allow him to broadcast to make sure that he adheres to providing this public with professional journalistic reporting. As the statements made by him leaves this family's values and reputation questioned, our telephone rings constantly from individuals who are concerned but more so from those who apparently have made judgments in this matter. I ask that all Virgin Islanders who have had similar experiences with Lee Carl and those of us who believe in truth and equality, to make an outcry to those responsible for Lee Carl's continued unprofessional broadcasts over the public airwaves. Our families do not have immunity from rumors but are destroyed by them.

What does his actions say to our children, our community, and to those who listen nationwide? He is a disgrace to the professional reporters here in these Virgin Islands. Let us stop this reoccurring situation. This grand standing by newsbreaks that are actually news fakes.

My fellow Virgin Islanders speak now or forever hold your peace.

Hurt, Angry and Pissed
The Williams Family

In the Virgin Islands we reward the wrongdoers and punish the law-abiding people. A cursory glance of the monuments bearing the names of the various honorees gives credence to what I have just said. Most if not all of these people are responsible for the way we live today. These are the same people who (a) continue to demand mediocrity, (b) have failed to lead by example, and (c) are responsible for our undisciplined society wherein the young men are busy killing each other. They are the only people that I know who can solve our problems with the same minds that created it. And by the way, while I'm being critical of certain people with good reason it behooves me to interject the following: As a retired sportscaster I have written two books, one entitled "Perpetuating the Memory of a Sportscaster" and the other entitled "The Sequel." Professional ethics being what it is, among radio and television personalities and with so many sportscasters and sports analysts in the Virgin Islands one would think that they would either privately or publicly congratulate me for having the courage to write these books dealing with truth. Knowing them as well as I do however, I feel safe in saying that they all should be charged with conduct unbecoming a sportscaster and or analyst. It is something that one should take to heart when consideration is given to the sad plight of our children. The logical question is, are they to grow up disrespecting each other because of jealousy and envy? In the Virgin Islands beginning with Melvin H. Evans (the first elected governor), no governor wants to play the hand he has been dealt.

As a former employee of the Virgin Islands Bureau of Internal Revenue who has written "The Extreme Test," the special report that follows, published by The Daily News on January 14, 1998, failed to startle me. Unlike the masses who continue to see the powers that be at the Bureau of Internal Revenue attired in the Emperor's New Clothes I (as a member of a minority group) know that there are no clothes and therefore the Emperor is naked. Having said that, I now direct your attention to The Daily News Report.

The Daily News, Wednesday, January 14, 1998

Audit hits collection at IRB

By WILL JONES
Daily News Staff

ST. CROIX — The Internal Revenue Bureau failed to collect nearly $12 million in taxes during the 1995 and 1996 fiscal years, according to a federal audit report.

The report by the U.S. Interior Department's inspector general indicated that the uncollected amount included $10.1 million in accounts receivable, $700,000 in bounced checks, $795,000 in improper penalty waivers and $324,000 because of the statute-of-limitation laws.

The report blamed many of the problems on the bureau's outdated computer system because taxpayers' complete histories could not be accessed from a single computer system; the lack of trained senior auditors; and the failure to file liens against properties owned by delinquent taxpayers.

The audit covered Oct. 1, 1994, through April 30, 1996, in which the bureau collected $515 million. About 90 percent of that amount represented gross receipts and income taxes.

Auditors found 12,410 delinquent income tax accounts, totaling $82.4 million for tax years 1978 to 1995.

Delinquent gross receipts tax accounts numbered 15,875 for a total of $9.6 million for tax years 1994 and 1995, the audit indicated.

The report also said the government owed $68.4 million in income tax refunds for 1994 and 1995 and that 11,200 returns from those years had not been processed.

It indicated that the Schneider administration had not responded to a draft of the report and that recommendations made by auditors were unresolved.

Internal Revenue Bureau Director Joseph Aubain did not return a call Tuesday to his St. Thomas office for comments on the report.

Also, the audit said the bureau lost $700,000 on 921 bounced checks because records were not changed to reflect that the bank had not honored the check.

"Accordingly, taxpayer accounts receivable were understated," the report said.

It also indicated that the bureau lost $11.2 million because the Delinquent Accounts and Return Bureau did not effectively use collection practices or tools to enforce the collection of money owed.

The losses were $10.5 million out of $15.2 million due from 1,750 returns, $324,0000 because the statute of limitation expired and $795,000 in penalties.

It said the bureau could lose another $940,000 within

▼ See **AUDIT**, page 2

AUDIT CONTINUED FROM PAGE ONE

Report offers ways to improve collections at IRB

the next two years unless collection actions are taken.

Hurricane Marilyn in September 1995 also cost the V.I. treasury millions of dollars in casualty losses.

As of September 1996, 537 people had filed loss claims totaling $15.2 million and were due $1.7 million in refunds, the report said.

During a March 4, 1997, meeting with bureau officials, auditors were told that the casualty claims had jumped to $75 million.

Recommendations included:

• Ensure that employees in the Delinquent Accounts and Return Bureau follow up with all taxpayers within 10 days after a taxpayer misses a specific payment deadline.

• Revenue officers maintain a master inventory listing of case histories for each taxpayer assigned to them.

• Enforce the V.I. Code on using liens and levies as collection tools.

• Grant penalty waivers only in accordance with regulations.

• The Legislature appropriate funds for the bureau to hire qualified senior revenue agents to conduct audits of the casualty claims and complex tax issues.

Two and a half years later, like the far-off rumble of thunder, coupe d'état action forced Governor Charles W. Turnbull to relieve Claudette Farrington of her responsibilities as director, replacing her with Louis M. Willis (the same law-breaking man who was exposed to you in "The Extreme Test"), prompting the Virgin Islands Independent Newspaper to write the following Editorial dated July 8, 2000.

Virgin Islands Independent, July 8, 2000

EDITORIAL:

Shootout at the BIR

The week's fun began on Wednesday, when Claudette Farrington was suddenly relieved of her duties at the Bureau of Internal Revenue. She was "reassigned" by the Gentle Giant to the Office of Management and Budget, a move known in corporate circles as a lateral pirouette.

Farrington was shown the gate at BIR literally hours before she was to have been grilled by Sen. Lorraine Berry's Finance Committee, a hearing to which she had been subpoenaed along with 19 other BIR supervisors. (There are 19 other BIR supervisors? Who's left to get supervised?)

Eyebrows shot due north when the governor's office announced the action, which came, as all government announcements do, late in the afternoon — which presumably gives the officials involved time to get out of the office and to the cover of home so the press doesn't get too stroppy. At least not until the next morning.

The inevitable questions popped up like targets on a shooting range. Why did the governor choose the 11th hour to sack Farrington? Why indeed did he sack her at all? Why didn't Senator Berry ignore the lateral pirouette and call Farrington onto the carpet anyway? Was a deal struck between Government House and Berry's committee in order to avoid embarrassment? And why did the senator and the new "acting" director of the BIR, Louis Willis, meet with Turnbull in executive (meaning closed to the stroppy press) session?

On his radio show, Sam Topp mused over some of these questions Friday morning, and it didn't take long for Senator Berry to phone in and explain, sort of, what happened. Why she did not respond to reporters' calls on the day before is not clear, but when she heard some unkind observations on the radio she became instantly available to clear the air. Problem is, she didn't clear the air. From what we think we heard is that she was going to get to the bottom of the BIR's problems, but now she would have to question Willis — and to be fair she had to give him time to get his ducks in a row.

But wait! Willis was, before he got his vertical pirouette, chief of collections at the very same department, BIR. So why does he get a few weeks to figure out what's going on when he has been in the BIR boat all this time? Very curious, indeed.

We do not mean to criticize Senator Berry, especially during French Heritage Week (comme il faut), since her head must be in as much of a spin as ours. But we would like to know why she let Farrington off the hook, why she didn't at least have an open-to-the-public chat with Willis and why she felt compelled to go into a smoke-filled room with the governor. If the intention was to raise the suspicions of the polity that a deal was being cut, it worked in spades.

Stay tuned for next week's exciting episode of this riveting soap opera. Since the BIR is the office to which we send a very large chunk of our wages every year, it might be helpful to find out what the Sam Hill is going on.

Eight years later it was (as they say) déjà vu all over again. Read for yourself this special report taken from the Daily News of January 25, 2008:

The Daily News, Friday, January 25, 2008

www.virginislandsdailynews.com

The Virgin Islands
DAILY 77 NEWS
A Pulitzer Prize-winning newspaper

FRIDAY, JANUARY 25, 2008   1 dollar

SPECIAL REPORT
Blistering U.S. audit finds disastrous V.I. tax collections
$253 million lost
Feds blame incompetence, favoritism and flagrant abuse of power as causes

By TIM FIELDS
Daily News Staff

Incompetence, favoritism and "flagrant abuse of power," have pervaded the V.I. government's tax collection agencies, costing the territory more than $253 million in uncollected taxes and prompting a federal criminal probe.

The V.I. Internal Revenue Bureau and Finance Department failed to collect more than $253 million in taxes over the last 10 years because of a chronic breakdown in their collection of delinquent taxes and through flagrant abuses of power by former government officials, according to a blistering U.S. Office of the Inspector General audit released this week.

"The Bureau of Internal Revenue and the Department of Finance did not act in the best interest of your government, doing very little to collect the taxes owed," Michael Colombo, Regional Audit Manager of the Office of the Inspector General, said in a Jan. 10 letter to Gov. John deJongh Jr.

The uncollected $253 million is more than the budgets for the Department of Education, the University of the Virgin Islands and the Board of Education combined in Fiscal Year 2008.

Of that $253 million, about $128 million of the taxes never can be recovered because some debts are so old, the audit reported.

Between 1997 and 2007, Colombo said, the process of collecting delinquent property, personal and corporate income and gross receipts taxes — was "inefficient and ineffectual, and does not fully comply with the law."

No assurances

In September 2006, the federal Inspector General launched a nine-month review of IRB and Finance — the two V.I. agencies primarily responsible for the collection of taxes for the General Fund.

IRB collects personal income taxes and corporate income, payroll withholdings, gross receipts and hotel occupancy taxes.

Finance collects real property taxes and sewer fees.

"Our evaluation disclosed significant internal control deficiencies that called into question the accuracy of the taxes owed," the audit reported.

IRB and Finance failed to assess taxpayers in a timely basis, failed to identify non-filers, failed to meet collection timelines and failed to focus collection efforts to maximize recovery of money owed, the audit reported.

"We also found agency practices that circumvent-

ed legislation enacted to prevent tax evasion through the use of tax clearance letters and the abuse of position by an official charged with enforcing the legislation," Colombo said.

He said the failure demonstrates a systematic breakdown in the collection of delinquent taxes, which undermines the integrity of the Virgin Islands tax system.

Clearance letters

Tax clearance letters are the territory's main weapon against tax evasion because every applicant for a business license must obtain a favorable clearance letter from IRB before the Department of Licensing and Consumer Affairs can issue the business a license.

However, IRB issued favorable clearance letters even though taxes were owed, and DLCA approved business licenses when letters were not present or unfavorable.

"These practices rendered the tax evasion legislation ineffective and further undermined the integrity" of the V.I. government's tax collection efforts,"

See IRB AUDIT, page 3

43

The Daily News, Friday, January 25, 2008 (cont.)   **SPECIAL REPORT**

IRB AUDIT
CONTINUED FROM THE FRONT PAGE

Colombo said.

The audit reported that the former IRB director issued more than 237 false tax clearance letters.

While not identified in the audit report, former director Louis Willis served in that position from September 2001 until the end of the administration of Gov. Charles Turnbull.

"Between 2002 and 2006, the former Director issued 237 favorable tax clearance letters to taxpayers, some of whom were not current in their filing and paying of taxes or did not have a payment agreement in place," the audit reported.

The letters falsely stated that the taxpayers were current in filing and paying their tax obligations, "thereby allowing them to evade payment of taxes to the GVI," Colombo said.

Willis issued 31 favorable tax clearance letters to a business person who owns 31 gas stations and convenient stores on St. Croix — and who owed $1.75 million in taxes.

"The businessperson had evaded filing and payment of taxes to the St. Croix office for seven years, despite efforts by a revenue officer and managers in that office to collect the taxes through summons, director returns, liens, and levies," the audit reported.

"When the management of the St. Croix office refused to issue favorable tax clearance letters to the businessperson, the businessperson traveled to St. Thomas, where the former Director issued favorable letters in May 2004 for a one-time payment of $25,000."

The audit report did not name the businessman.

The Inspector General has referred this abuse by the former director to its Office of Investigations, the audit reported.

The audit also cited another instance, which occurred in 2002, when an IRB supervisor issued an unfavorable tax clearance letter to an unidentified contractor who owed $435,000 in delinquent taxes.

The former director disregarded that letter, issued a favorable one, and then continued to issue favorable letters to the same contractor through 2005 — even though the contractor owed the government $437,000 in delinquent gross receipts and withholding taxes, the audit found.

The audit report did not name the contractor.

Licensing and Consumer Affairs further weakened the point of tax clearance letters by issuing business licenses without such documentation.

The auditors found eight instances where applicants received current business licenses without obtaining a tax clearance letter and three other instances where, despite unfavorable tax clearance letters, applicants were granted current business licenses.

Daily News Photo by NICK SCHNEEMAN

The V.I. Internal Revenue Bureau comes under searing criticism in a new federal audit.

In one instance, an applicant with $3.5 million in unpaid gross receipts and withholding taxes still was given a business license, the audit reported.

"We were told that DLCA, acting alone and contrary to the law, established an internal policy that allows only 15 working days for receipt of a tax clearance letter before DLCA will issue a license anyway," the audit report states. "This practice creates an environment that at best fails to prevent tax evasion and at worst encourages and abets it."

Persistent problems

"The failure to address identified long-standing deficiencies in the collection of delinquent taxes continues a decade-long practice of administrative non-feasance," the audit report states.

The $253 million in delinquent taxes include:
- $88.7 million in personal and corporate income
- $73.6 million in gross receipts
- $61.4 million in property
- $27.7 million in payroll withholding
- $2 million in hotel occupancy

Since the debts span 10 years, $128 million is not likely to be collected, which is a potential waste of financial resources that could have been used by the government, the audit reported.

Under V.I. law, IRB must assess taxes within three years after a return is filed. If an assessment is not made within three years, IRB cannot legally collect the tax.

"The older the debt, the less likely it will be collected," the audit reported.

IRB did not initiate collection processes until an average of 18 months after returns were filed, which significantly reduced its ability to collect money owed, the audit found.

Even when assessments were made, IRB failed to send out second and third delinquency notices within 90 days. Those notices serve as a reminder to the taxpayer that payment is due and that property could be seized.

IRB's system to generate the notices was disabled in 2004 because of insufficient capacity on the computer system and because a large number of errors occurred during a changeover from an older computer system.

Because IRB discontinued issuing second and third notices, the tax system no longer generated delinquency reports. "Without these reports, the Chief of Delinquent Accounts and Returns stated that she began assigning cases based on high dollar values," the audit reports states.

That was not what happened, however. Cases were not assigned to revenue officers systematically.

"In fact, of the 160 taxpayer accounts reviewed, 109, valued at $13.7 million, had never been assigned to revenue officers for collection, although some had been assessed as far back as 1997," the audit report states.

IRB also ineffectively used revenue officers by allocating them other time-consuming duties, such as researching the validity of taxpayer delinquencies, instead of using the officers solely for enforcement of collections and identification of non-filers

For example:
- A contractor owed $960,190 in withholding taxes from March 2002 through April 2007. Failure to pay withholding taxes can lead to imprisonment. However, after years of IRB action, the liens were rendered unenforceable.
- A hotel owed $100,000 in occupancy taxes since 2000. However, it was not until 2006, when IRB found out the property was going to be sold, that IRB prepared a summons and a lien, but it

44

The Daily News, Friday, January 25, 2008 (cont.)

was too late. The property was sold for $200,00, and IRB was unable to collect the $100,000 in taxes.

• A doctor currently in business has filed only one withholding tax return — in 2002.

The audit reported that IRB has failed to make any effort to ensure that wage earners, including many government employees, paid their taxes — even though IRB had all the information it needed to enforce the collections.

"We found that 18,669 W-2 and 1099 information returns for tax years 2003 and 2004, representing over $221 million in wages, could not be matched to any filed tax returns," the audit reported.

"Of those filers, 5,609 W-2s and 1099s were related to GVI employees, with reported earnings of over $83 million," the audit report said.

Although IRB was aware of the non-filers, "it did not take action to ensure that they filed or that appropriate penalties were applied to the accounts," the audit found.

Real property taxes

The audit report also found that the Finance Department's efforts to collect property taxes were ineffective.

The audit found that Finance used antiquated recordkeeping practices that could not provide up-to-date taxpayer information and that Finance exerted minimal effort to collect unpaid taxes.

Finance enforcement officers must sift by hand through old bills kept in file cabinets and piled on shelves, the auditors noted.

"This time-consuming process hindered collection efforts because enforcement officers and collectors had to allocate a significant amount of time to researching taxpayer delinquencies rather than actually collecting taxes," the audit reported.

The auditors also found understaffing, especially in the Finance Department's St. Croix office.

They also identified an area of possible misuse of funds on contractors who may have been no-show workers.

"We were told that retired enforcement officers were contracted to prepare and issue status reports to delinquent taxpayers. However, we were unable to determine what, if anything, was done by these contractors because DOF could not locate documentation showing their efforts," the audit report states.

Like IRB, Finance has a dismal record of collections.

Since 2005, Finance has not had a sale of property to satisfy tax debt.

"These efforts fall far short of what is needed to recover the delinquent property tax debt of $61.4 million," the audit reported.

— *Contact Tim Fields at 774-8772 ext. 364 or e-mail tfields@dailynews.vi.*

In Chapter 2 of this book as an aside I listed for your information the names of Fred Clarke and John Collins, two white men who were altruistic and brave enough in showing the whole wide world how I (a sixth generation St. Thomian) was being persecuted by our ancestral natives and native Virgin Islanders for working in accordance with the law. The point that I'm making here is that my compatriots (apathetic and timid as they are) would never say anything positive about the things I was forced to endure as an employee of the Virgin Islands Government. They will sing the praises of Rothschild Francis because he is dead. Liston Monsanto (alive and well) having defeated the Virgin Islands Governmental System must wait until he dies to receive credit for a job well done. As long as you are not a threat to the oppressors you are glorified. This abrasive attitude as displayed in our society is a conspicuous example of hypocrisy. We act most of the time in an aimless confused manner. Having said that, what's worthy of note is that following my retirement from government I wrote the following editorial which appeared in The Daily News of July 13, 2001:

Opinion

A view inside government

Liston Monsanto lives on St. Thomas.

I begin this editorial by paraphrasing the Roman political leader Brutus: Not that I love the politicians and the many people who have occupied positions of authority over the last 30 years less, but that I love the Virgin Islands more.

I find it of the utmost importance to communicate via this newspaper with the many disadvantaged people in the U.S. Virgin Islands whose tendencies to remain in a fixed condition without change continue to be exploited by members of the "establishment" and their toadies.

When I served the people of the Virgin Islands as an employee of the government, I found out that the noblest form of leadership came not by example but through nepotism and discrimination. Now it is neither my intention to wage a contentious campaign against anyone nor is it my intention in any way, shape, or form to seize the reigns of the Virgin Islands government.

Nevertheless, having preserved the memory of life therein and seeing first-hand the improper and hurtful treatment given to many of the "faceless trolls" who were courting the favor of the "establishment" as a winner.

My victory Opinion No. 81-1434, 3rd Circuit Court had a wide-ranging impact on the intelligence community. It meant that outside talent when compared to home-grown talent (while not superior) was indeed free from personal feelings or prejudice when it became necessary to make an impartial decision; the power elite in the Virgin Islands, who did not know the difference between truth and falsehood, had been defeated; that limited as my education was, I had succeeded in doing what those who were formally educated had been afraid to do; and that the precedent-setting case for succeeding generations and every person (with or without a resume) presently under the American flag.

As a paragon of efficiency I have always believed that little things accomplished are far better than big things talk about. Moreover, I believe that willful and open disrespect should not be tolerated by any decent human being.

Liston Monsanto

An employee working in a manner reflective of his training and ability has to be exceptionally strong or exceptionally stupid. Why? Because following our right to elect our governor in 1970, the power elite (given greater autonomy)

> ##
>
> **And while we are shamming over ethnocentrism and xenophobia, we have built a Virgin Islands society for everybody except those of us who were born here.**

entered into a covenant with mediocrity which immediately replaced skill and strategy with arbitrary power. This aberrant behavior on the part of the many trained and educated people created a political system and collaboration in tandem with each other, they would contrive and arrange by agreement to place underachievers and unlettered people in key positions, thereby creating a less than professional atmosphere throughout the territory.

Here in the Virgin Islands we find ourselves in a sordid mess. Our people are influenced more by impulse than by reason. As a matter of fact, it has been said that the subject of work in the Virgin Islands government has to be treated with a measure of caution inasmuch as working in an environment where loyalty is more important than honesty and where just about everyone is indifferent to corruption does nothing to enhance the credibility of that environment.

The principle of letting people do as they please (laissez faire) has become the order of the day. Through spurious relationships, craft and hypocrisy, many trained and educated people in positions of authority are able to operate perfunctorily. Trained employees find themselves coordinating their work with half-trained and untrained employees. For reasons known only to the trained employees, they refuse to demand better or to otherwise apply the lessons learned in the various institutions of learning.

Our attitudes and overall lifestyle on these small islands of pretending to like each other evoke memories of the seven deadly sins of the world, and transcends disbelief to a stranger.

And while we are shamming over ethnocentrism and xenophobia, we have built a Virgin Islands society for everybody except those of us who were born here. The business-like attitude needed in carrying out the government's business is entirely absent. Most people are coming to the Virgin Islands in search of their pound of flesh. Like many of us, very few are concerned with what they can do for the Virgin Islands. Money leaves the territory in union dues, Puerto Rican Lottery, taxicab fares, Medical Air Services, etc. With less than professional attitudes, we continue to reflect the environment in which we are trained.

The Internal Revenue Bureau, which is the mirror image of the U.S. Internal Revenue Service, has become an inferior entity as it cannot operate in a vacuum without any concern for the other departmental agencies. Health care and education are also affected by the aforementioned covenant and the lack of strict enforcement laws, brought about by laissez-faire, has landed many of our children in jail.

It saddens me to see that the trained and educated people in management whom we thought would deliver us from most of the prevailing evil on our march to utopia would leave us leaderless. Instead of helping and providing leadership that's so desperately needed, they become exasperated owing to anybody's willingness to help a fallen brother or sister. They somehow fail to see that there are many advantages in following the law. They continue to be politically correct, but dead wrong.

Because my home was all cluttered with old newspapers and other odds and ends and because Hurricanes Hugo and Marilyn ravaged many parts of my property, it was a most difficult task collating my material for this book; consequently it could not be written in chronological order. The above was used as a preface to say that following the editorial you've just read, I made a trip off island and almost by happenstance upon my return I picked up The Daily News of August 2, 2001. Therein I found the following opinion from Mr. Charles Starr, another white person.

Daily News August 2, 2001

Opinion   **27**

Things are not like they use to be or like they will be

Charles Starr, a Water Island resident, is a Daily News contributing columnist.

Recently The Daily News published a guest column by Liston Monsanto in which he reprised a courageous stand he took 25 years ago. His intent, I'm sure, was not to pat himself on the back, but to give his thoughts about things changing during his lifetime in ways that disturb him.

I've read the 3rd Circuit Court's opinion of Mr. Monsanto's case and it is an astounding record of a journey he began at a time when it was unfashionable to take on the system.

Beginning in late 1975, Monsanto, an employee of the then Tax Division, became concerned about the way the department was being run. He wrote letters to his superiors and sent copies of some of them the governor and the lieutenant governor. His complaints covered inefficiency, poor management, low morale among employees, ineffective tax collecting measures and at least one case of an employee filing fraudulent tax returns.

Monsanto's superiors apparently became impatient and warned him that if he didn't stop he'd be penalized. The GESC rejected the recommendation that he be fired and settled on a 90-day suspension without pay. In their letter to him and in their response to the GESC his bosses cited his attempts to tarnish the image of the Tax Division, writing malicious letters, character assassination, using government stationary and supplies to write his letters, hand-delivering the letters during business hours, not working a full eight hours each day and having "released (his) letters to the media." Monsanto lost the appeal with the GESC and lost on appeal in a district court.

His attorney took the case to the 3rd Circuit Court and won. In their opinion on March 11, 1982, the court said, in so many words, that the findings of the GESC and the charges against Monsanto, including the alleged release of his letters to the media, were a crock. He'd

Charles Starr

been wrongfully suspended and his rights to protected free speech were violated.

Mr. Monsanto showed great courage and the record is there for all to see. However, in his otherwise poignant article he wondered why we couldn't return to the way things used to be before the Virgin Islands elected its first governor.

❝

Change is inevitable but only if the people demand it. Mr. Monsanto demanded it and made our islands a little bit better.

He seems to believe that it was a telling time in what would become a terrible slide toward disaster. He's correct yet the worst would not come until the election of the three predecessors to Charles Turnbull whose administrations might charitably be called flaccid at best.

There are two concerns Monsanto discusses to which I'd like to react. He says that outsiders come to our islands and seek their "pound of flesh." Of course we've had more than our share of con artists who come in, harvest the goodies and duck out. Recall the fly-by-night contractors who descended like vultures in the aftermath of Hugo and Marilyn. And don't believe for a minute that there are not some business people and government employees out there still waiting for the chance to pounce.

The truth of the matter is that many

people who were not born here established honest businesses and contribute to our well being. Not only do they run their businesses well within accepted good ethical practices, they support, out of pocket, a great many community activities. Their contribution to our economic and social lives is immeasurable.

As for creating a Virgin Islands society for everyone but those who were born here, I'd ask Mr. Monsanto to reflect on how we got into the mess in the first place. I won't argue for a minute that the problems we are confronted with each day are not apparent, but I'd ask him to think about who it was that got us in that state. Many, perhaps most, were born here and some of them took advantage of a burgeoning system that became ripe for picking.

Others simply don't give a damn. There is no better example than that of 10 senators who, only weeks ago, told the voters that they couldn't care less that two-thirds of them said clearly during the November referendum that they wanted the size of the Senate reduced. It's the perfect example of someone being given 10 options to solve a problem, but never failing to pick the worst one. But was it not the same voters who put them in office to begin with? Go figure.

Weak government in all forms is as old as history itself. It's a fact of life and will remain so, but to realize it should not imply acceptance. Change is inevitable but only if the people demand it. Mr. Monsanto demanded it and made our islands a little bit better.

It would be nice to return to less complicated times, but it's not in the cards. I would love to return to the idyllic little farming community in southern New Jersey where I was born and raised. But it no more resembles the remnant memories of my youth than those of the Virgin Islands of Mr. Monsanto's youth. The utopia he longs for is only a dream.

One can try to nourish it and strive toward it, but in the final analysis it will remain a dream far removed from reality.

Mr. Starr's "opinion" was presumably written with a view towards impressing and influencing other fair-minded people. He knew then as he knows today that one has one of three ways of living his life: (a) the lawful way, (b) the unlawful way, and (c) the utopian way which went out with the Garden of Eden. Anyway, I had to thank Mr. Starr -- a man I have yet to meet -- for his sincerity and heartfelt comments. Accordingly on August 2, 2001 I sent him this letter.

August 2, 2001

Mr. Charles Starr
Contributing Columnist
The Daily News
9155 Estate Thomas
St. Thomas, U.S. Virgin Islands 00802

Dear Mr. Starr:

Jackie Robinson (the man who broke Baseball's color barrier) once said: "If I had a room jammed with trophies, awards, and citations, and a child of mine came to me into that room and asked what I had done in defense of black people and decent whites fighting for freedom - and I had to tell that child I had kept quiet, that I had been timid, I would have to mark a total failure in the whole business of living." This quotation may give you a clue as to what kind of person I am.

Ordinarily, I'd respond via telephone to your unbiased column which appears in The Daily News of August 2, 2001, by simply saying thank you, but when a man says something that hasn't been said in 25 years, it deserves more than a cursory notice. So, to you I express my gratitude and pleasure over your detailed expansion of my article which appeared in the Daily News of July 13, 2001.

As they say, what is past is prologue. And so without belaboring the point, I'd like to say that with respect to the so-called "Outsiders" and their "pound of flesh" of which both of us spoke, please be informed that our paths have not diverged. The gist of my article was essentially designed to say exactly what you said in your column. You obviously misread. That being said, your feelings accord with mine. Again, many thanks. "All's well that ends well," as Shakespeare once wrote.

Very truly yours,

Liston B. Monsanto, Sr.
P.O. Box 2763
St. Thomas, V.I. 00803
(340) 774-4199

c.c. The Daily News

As I write, crime in the Virgin Island has reached epidemic proportions. Like the Wild West shots are being fired from every nook and cranny and gunfights have become commonplace as people continue to fear for their lives. Like a guttered candle with the melted wax running down its side, people are wondering when it will all melt away. Inasmuch as the young men on the Islands feel no fears in the midst of battle, many of our residents have become paralyzed with fear and horror.

For those readers with a spasmodic interest in reading who have not yet read the other books authored by me and now find it a most difficult task assimilating the contents of this book, I earnestly ask that you think it over with a view towards educating those people in the United States Virgin Islands -- many of whom have a propensity for twisting things to their own desire while continuing to bluff their way through life.

For me to write a book favoring a Virgin Islands totalitarian governmental system which I defeated through Opinion Number 81-1434 of the Third Circuit Court would be as bad as it gets, and, moreover, an abandonment of my principles and a desertion of my cause.

In conclusion, let me say that my purpose in this book is not to upstage anybody but, rather, to show the reader how nonpartisan I am as a voter and resident of the United States Virgin Islands.

Brothers and Sisters: You were once in darkness, but now you are light in the Lord. Live as Children of the Light, for Light, produces every kind of goodness and Righteousness and Truth. Try to Learn what is Pleasing to the Lord. Take no part in the Fruitless works of Darkness; Rather Expose them, for it is shameful even to mention the things done by them in secret; but everything exposed by the light becomes visible is Light. Therefore; it says "Awake O Sleeper, and arise from the Dead, and Christ will give you Light."

Ephesians 5: 8-14

Liston B. Monsanto, Sr., is a man of deep faith and integrity. Like many of the oppressors in the U.S. Virgin Islands, he has children of whom he's very proud. Due largely to his rigid impartiality he is considered evil by the power elite and a number of ingrates who continue to smart over Opinion Number 81-1434 of the 3rd Circuit Court of Appeals. Together with his wife, Wilma, he continues to live in St. Thomas, Virgin Islands.